LEVERAGE

HOW TO ACCELERATE THE
SPEED & VELOCITY
OF YOUR RESULTS

BY
ERIC LOFHOLM
AUTHOR OF
THE SYSTEM, DUPLICATION, AND *FOCUS*
JAMES KARL BUTLER
AUTHOR OF
THE SYSTEM IS THE SECRET AND *FOCUS*

DEDICATION:

To entrepreneurs and sales professionals who seek to utilize the powerful principle of leverage to accelerate the speed and velocity at which they get things done

This publication is designed to provide accurate and authoritative information in regard to the subject matter covered. It is sold with the understanding that the publisher is not engaged in rendering legal, accounting, or other professional service. If legal advice or other expert assistance is required, the services of a professional should be sought.

Lofholm, Eric, and Butler, James Karl
Focus: The Key Skill to Igniting Your Productivity
ISBN-13: 978-1508573586
ISBN-10: 1508573581
1. Business
2. Productivity

LEVERAGE
HOW TO ACCELERATE THE SPEED & VELOCITY OF YOUR RESULTS

"Give me a lever long enough and a fulcrum on which to place it, and I shall move the world."—Archimedes

To understand the principle of leverage, consider this story that is found in Brian Tracy's book *Victory* that illustrates the power of leverage and in this particular case during World War II of something the Allies knew that helped them defeat the German army.

"The Germans...had a secret weapon, the Enigma machine. This incredibly sophisticated device allowed the Germans to communicate worldwide with a code that was impossible to break. Each encoded message was encrypted differently from each subsequent message when it was run through the Enigma machine. Because of this, there was no consistent code to be broken by the Allied powers. The German intelligence services and military commanders could send and receive top-secret messages worldwide with no fear of detection.

"However, an incredibly fortunate event took place early in the war. The Allies were able to obtain an Enigma machine and secretly transport it into England. The existence of this machine in Allied intelligence became one of the biggest secrets of the war and was not revealed until well after the war was over.

"The Allies set up a separate intelligence unit at a large estate called Bletchley Park forty miles north of London. This unit was fully staffed by intelligence experts with the highest top-secret clearances possible in the Allied military. These code-breakers and translators worked day and night throughout the entire war intercepting German communications, deciphering them, and making them available to the key commanders and relevant parties.

"This intelligence breakthrough was a major reason for the Allied victory in Europe. The capture of an Enigma machine and the codebooks that went with it gave the Allies a critical edge that enabled them to ultimately prevail over a formidable military force....Sometimes, one piece of information is all that is necessary to give the advantage to one force or the other." –Brian Tracy, *Victory*, pp. 102-103.

What kind of power or leverage would you have if you knew what your competitors would do before they did it?

Obviously, we can't have that exact power, but thinking about the story of the Engima machine, helps you understand the power of anticipating what others will do and then acting on that knowledge. Such knowledge gives you a tremendous edge or leverage point over them.

A more valuable question is: What kind of power or leverage would you have if you could think about and anticipate shifts in the market before they happened?

Such information would be invaluable. The important point from both of these questions is that leverage gives you an advantage. In this short book, we're going to share leverage points with you to help you gain the advantage in your market niche. To do so, consider the best assets you have in your business and carefully consider how you can better leverage them to help you get what you want.

A good way to understand the concept of leverage is to look at the character of Mickey Mouse. Mickey Mouse was originally a cartoon character used in short cartoons in movie theatres. Since then, that same asset has been leveraged many ways through comic books, books, videos, movies, cartoons, clothing, toys, theme parks, a cable TV network, and licensing for untold numbers of products. You can see how one idea has been leveraged across a wide variety of media to get even more benefit and value than was originally thought when the character was just a drawing on a page.

This is such an important idea because very few business owners in general really understand how to leverage their assets for maximum benefit. Our goal in this short book is to help you understand better how you can leverage what you already have to help you build and expand your brand.

To begin, it will be helpful to better understand the definition of word leverage. The dictionary defines leverage as the exertion of force by means of a lever . This is done because a mechanical advantage is gained in this way. Another definition defines leverage as the power to influence a person or situation to achieve a particular outcome.

A third definition says that leverage is the act of financing the ratio of a company's loan capital (debt) to the value of its common stock (equity).

A brilliant explanation of the concept of leverage is found in Robert Kiyosaki 's book entitled *Retire Young, Retire Rich*. The book is all about the types of leverage that business owners can use to grow their businesses.

In the introduction, Robert Kiyosaki makes this statement: "Leverage is the reason some people become rich and others do not become rich....Because leverage is power, some use it, some abuse it, and others fear it." –*Retire Young, Retire Rich*, p. xiii.

He continues:
"The reason less than 5 percent of all Americans are rich is because only 5 percent know how to *use* the power of leverage. Many who want to become rich, fail to become rich because they *abuse* the power. And most people do not become rich because they *fear* the power of leverage."

He also defines leverage as the ability to do more with less. He says:

"In the broad definition of the word, the word leverage simply means the ability to do more with less. When it came to the subject of work, money, and leverage, rich dad would say, 'If you want to become rich, you need to work less, and earn more. In order to do that, you employ some form of leverage.' He contrasted that statement by saying, 'People who only work hard have limited leverage. If you're working hard physically and not getting ahead financially, then you're probably someone else's leverage.'" –*Retire Young, Retire Rich*, p. 33.

There are numerous examples of leverage. Here are a few:
- o   Fishing – bare hands vs. fishing pole vs. net
- o   Other people's money (Debt)
- o   Other people's time (Employment of others)
- o   Other people's relationships (Ask yourself: Who already has a relationship with the prospect you want to sell to?)
- o   Time (How do you use your spare time? How you use your time affects what happens as a result. For instance, you can choose to use well the time that others waste. It is easy to assign priority to things that don't help you achieve your goals. You can choose to spend an hour watching television, shopping, reading, or working on something that builds your business. How you leverage your time influences how quickly you will grow.)

Now, let's consider the definition of an asset, specifically in the context of how that asset can be used as leverage. The dictionary has two definitions for the word asset. These are:
- A useful or valuable thing, person, or quality; *quick reflexes were his chief asset   The school is an asset to the community*
- Property owned by a person or company, regarded as having value and available to meet debts, commitments or legacies: *growth in net assets*

Why is it important to understand the words "leverage" and "asset" in conjunction with growing your business?

The key is that you can't do it all alone through your own work. You have to create assets and leverage them to help you grow beyond your own capacity. Let's consider nine ways you can use leverage to help you build and expand your business and six multipliers that will give you a bigger crowbar so you can get more leverage.

1. Use the leverage of your mind to entertain the realm of possibility of how you can grow your business.
The most powerful leverage you have (regardless of the size of your business) is in your mind because you have to entertain the realm of possibility before you can embrace it as your new reality. This is why it is so important to associate with and learn from others who stretch your realities. They help you see what is possible (and grab onto those new realities like a crowbar that removes the obstacles) instead of being stuck in the same old ways of doing things.

Robert Kiyosaki makes this statement about leverage:
"The number one leverage is the leverage found in your mind because it is where you realities are formed."-p. 55.

The realities of our own minds can hold us back from accomplishing more. To help you understand this idea, consider the belief or reality that existed for many people before the Wright brothers helped others see that human beings could fly. The popular idea at the time was that "humans can't fly." It wasn't until the Wright brothers used the leverage of their minds to envision another possibility that they were willing to work to find a way. Once they embraced the new reality that it was possible to fly were they willing to step out and do something about it.

Another example is when Roger Bannister broke the 4-minute mile barrier. At the time, the popular belief and reality for most people was that it was impossible for any human being to run a four-minute mile. The reality that most people believed was that the human heart couldn't withstand such exertion and that it would explode if anyone attempted to run this fast. What is important about what Roger

Bannister did is that he believed he could break the four-minute mile before he did. He embraced this new reality in his mind and used the leverage of his mind to work and train so that he could break the four-minute mile. Then, once he did it and proved it was possible, numerous others were able to do it as well.

2. Understand and leverage the eleven assets you have in ways that help you maximize your potential and power.
To grow your business, you need to better leverage the assets you have. Your own individual assets aren't enough.

To help you better understand how you can leverage your business assets, I've listed the eleven biggest assets any business has (regardless of size) below. As you consider each of these assets, think about both sides of the leverage spectrum and why one business has more power and leverage than another with the same asset.

You should ask yourself questions to allow yourself to think about how to better leverage the assets you have particularly with the distinction of measuring your time in terms of results per hour. As you consider these questions, ask yourself: Where can I get more than an hour of results for an hour of results?

For example, if you record 2 podcasts per week over a period of five years and build your audience to a million listens (or downloads), the power of leverage will be that one hour of time can help me reach an audience of thousands, ten thousands, hundreds of thousands or millions of connections with prospective clients. The whole concept of leverage allows you to think differently.

Another example is around the principle of productivity. If you hire someone for $9/hour and they work 20 hours a week, you gain 80 hours per month in productivity.

Take the time to carefully think about this concept and how it relates to the assets you already have. You won't ever develop these assets and use them to gain more leverage unless you thing about how to expand them first. Then, and only then, will you move past belief to take action and develop these assets into better leverage points to launch your business to a higher level.

Asset	How Can You Better Leverage These?
1. Your brand identity and all of your intellectual property (business name, brand identity, logo, etc.)	Which has more power and leverage? • An individual or business that relies on the product lines of others to sell OR • An individual or business that builds his or her own brand and then leverages it in many ways. Why? How can you better leverage this asset at your business?
2. Your status as an authority figure, celebrity specialist	Who has more power and leverage in the your business niche? • A celebrity OR • You or any competitor that isn't well known or thought of as an expert or authority • The current leader in your market OR • Any business that tries to copy or mimic the leader Why?

		How can you better leverage this asset at your business?
3.	Your processes and systems	Which has more power and leverage? • No processes and systems OR • Well thought out processes and systems that anyone in your business can run (without you having to be there all of the time) Why? How can you better leverage this asset in your business?
4.	Your brand reputation in your market	Which has more power and leverage? • To be known for what you sell OR • To be known for the experience clients have when they work with you? Why? How can you better leverage this asset in your business?
5.	Your sales consultants and staff	Which has more power and leverage? • Well trained sales consultant who sells 3 out of every four prospects OR • Poorly trained sales consultant

	who sells 1 our of every four prospects Why? How can you better leverage this asset in your business?

6. Your clients (who have already purchased from you)	Which has more power and leverage?
	  • Business who is content with the sale they have just made to a client
	OR
	  • Business who consistently invites and sells to clients who buy from you and asks for referrals after every sale
	Why?
	
	How can you better leverage this asset in your business?

7. The exclusivity of what you sell in your market niche	Which has more power and leverage?
	  • Business with no exclusive products (they carry what everyone else and Internet vendors carry)?
	OR
	  • Business who carries what no one else has and what can't be found online
	Why?
	
	How can you better leverage this in your business?

8. Your connections (people clients in your area should know but don't)	Which has more power and leverage? • Business who introduces clients who buy from them to the top individuals or vendors in their area (and charges these vendors for this opportunity) OR • The business who knows top individuals and vendors, but doesn't take the time to introduce clients to them (because they are too busy or because clients will meet these individuals or vendors on their own) Why? How can you better leverage this asset in your business?
9. Investments (Inventory)	Which has more power and leverage? • Business with limited inventory or product line that doesn't have a lot of depth of selection OR • Business with depth of inventory or product line so prospects can find exactly what they are looking for Why? How can you better leverage this asset in your business?

10. Your relationships with key vendors and suppliers.	Which has more power and leverage? • Business who barely knows their key vendors OR • Business who really gets to know their key vendors and spends their time and money (through purchases) to build better relationships Who do you think gets more attention when challenges come up? How can you better leverage this asset in your business?
11. Toll positions – Will others pay you to be in front of your clients (who they want to sell to as well)?	Which has more power and leverage? • Business who gives access to their clients for free (handing out business cards and flyers to clients just because business owners dropped by) OR • Business who helps build bridge between their clients and the businesses that want to be in touch with those clients (and charge for the opportunity) Why? How can you better leverage this asset in your business?

3. Find and use multipliers which will give you a bigger crowbar and even more leverage.
A multiplier is something that allows you to increase the benefit you would get out of the same thing by looking at it differently. Well placed and executed multipliers can have a huge impact on the amount of leverage you can utilize in your business.

Here are six examples of multipliers which could provide leverage for your business:

1. **Unused capacity or unexploited opportunity**
This is a big multiplier because you can utilize your resources and untapped opportunities as a leverage points for your businesses.

Here are five examples of how this multiplier has changed industries in which it has been used to get you thinking about how to utilize this multiplier in your business.

1) Fast food
Ray Kroc, the founder of McDonalds was vehemently opposed to adding breakfast to their menu for years. He once famously said, "No one eats hamburgers for breakfast." However, today 45% of McDonald's revenue comes from breakfast AND it is the most profitable area of their business. They looked at how they could leverage their unused capacity, which in this case was by offering breakfast. That was a profitable decision for them at the time. Their re-invention of the coffee business through their McCafé expansion was a big hit for them and put Starbucks on the defensive for some time. It is a good idea for you to consider unexploited opportunities in your business. Where do you have capacity that is not currently being used? Could you expand and make this unexploited opportunity work for your business?

A big lesson can be learned from what coffee retailer Starbucks is currently experimenting with and exploring as it relates to the multiplier of unused capacity. Starbucks has found that 70% of all of their business is done before 2pm so they are looking for ways to expand their unused capacity in the afternoons and evenings. Their idea is to have Starbucks also be a wine bar where their customers can

come and order wine in the late afternoons and evening. They have been testing this idea in several markets. The test stores are designed to see if they can get their customers to respond to buying beer, wine and gourmet delicacies in the evenings at their stores (during a time when sales are traditionally flat). Many people don't think this is a very good idea, but Carol Tice at BNET in a recent article says: "The new wine-bar approach is a 'great strategy for developing a whole new after-work business. Independent coffeehouses have long morphed into wine bars when night falls, so this makes perfect sense. These are highly compatible businesses, and adding booze will allow Starbucks to grow its nighttime revenue, which currently is usually... nothing.'" Derek Thompson at *The Atlantic* adds: "Ordering beer at Starbucks... doesn't feel quite right — yet, but there's a real need for what they're offering. The demand for quieter alcohol-serving joints (that aren't sit-down restaurants where we'll feel guilty ordering only liquids) feels strangely underserved, and 'that's an argument for Starbucks'... strategy to work.' --
http://theweek.com/article/index/208383/starbucks-gamble-on-beer-and-wine-will-it-work

Starbucks used this multiplier by having locations at Barnes and Noble bookstores. Barnes and Noble could make money from renting the space to Starbucks and Starbucks could find new clients by creating a business within another business.

Where is there unused capacity or unexploited opportunity in your business?

Is there someone that you could align yourself with to expand your business in this way?

2) Television
Many children or teenagers today may find it hard to believe that it wasn't that long ago when TV went off the air at midnight. Today, television has found tremendous leverage by selling infomercial time during off peak hours to advertisers who want to sell their products

via stories and numerous testimonials. This is an example of unused capacity being found in time. Convenience stores and many other businesses have found unused capacity in time by opening their businesses to be open 24-hours.

3) Stored value - Making sales on the back-end to existing customers
What else do you have to sell that you could offer to existing clients?

Do you view your current prospects and clients as an opportunity of stored value? Could a new product, service, or offering be created to help existing clients do business with you again?

Auto insurance agents typically also sell home and life insurance. This is an example of tapping into the stored value of a client. Real estate agents know that people typically sell their home after an average of seven years. If they stay in contact with their home buyers, they may have opportunity to list or help their past client sell or find a new home.

What stored value currently exists in your business that you could better leverage with time?

4) Different distribution model
If you have a brick and mortar store, could you be selling your product or service online? If you sell online, is there an opportunity for you to consider new joint venture opportunities or affiliate programs to help you distribute what you sell in different ways and areas?

Such questions can help you discover new opportunities and multipliers to grow your business.

Harley Davidson noticed that from 1997 to 2007, the number of women motorcycle owners grew by 36% and that number is expected to double by the year 2017. Kathy Tolleson, CEO of Roar Motorcycles sees mass-affluent women buyers as the greatest opportunity for the motorcycle industry. She currently has her own e-Book, offers apparel, jewelry and its own cosmetic line (Windblown®) and custom makes motorcycles for women

(DreamBike®). She has grown her business to capitalize on this trend.

Could you grow your business by looking to expand or create an entirely different distribution model?

5) Unconverted leads - These are prospects who have been into your business or marketing funnel, but haven't purchased anything from you yet.
What systems will you put in place to ensure that you don't forget about these leads?

Neglecting to put a system in place to follow up with your unconverted leads is a big opportunity for most businesses. How would it change yours if you had a well-executed system of follow up and conversion?

As you've considered these five areas, what unused capacity or unexploited opportunities are there in your business that you could now capitalize on in the future?

-
-
-
-
-

2. Changing how you present your product and sell it to others.
If you are selling a low percentage of prospects coming into your business, you would benefit greatly by preselling your prospect. Here is an important question for you to consider: What are you providing to your prospects to prepare him or her to buy from you before they actually consider your offer?

Many Internet marketers use a process of creating three or four information based videos before they explain or release their offer. This gives a prospect a chance to build a relationship with the seller before the offer is made. If you meet with your prospects face to face in the sales process, you should send your prospects some form of "What to Expect" collateral to help that individual see why they should do business with you before they arrive.

For example, one plastic surgeon, deliberately delays any discover or discussion appointment with the prospect so that material can be sent and prospect can be pre-sold. In addition to a copy of the plastic surgeon's book (which positions her as an expert and an authority, her "What to Expect" packet includes information about some of the concerns or fears that the prospect may be feeling on different DVDs depending on the procedure to be performed. The DVDs showcase numerous testimonials of happy clients who have loved the experience. Then, prior to the appointment, a receptionist calls to follow up and give out some assignments before the prospect arrives to meet with the doctor. One of the assignments she checks is to ensure that the right DVD has been watched prior to her arrival. This will help pre-sell her on the procedure she is considering and answer her questions. It reduces the amount of time required for the sales appointment and most importantly the prospect is prepared to buy because the script on the DVD prepares the prospect to do so.

If you haven't already, you should write your own eBook or have your own "What to Expect" brochure that details what will happen and explains why you are the best choice for the product or service they are considering.

Another way, you can alter the means of selling is by selling experiences, not products. Consider how Disney builds the sale at their theme parks entirely around an experience and memories. Car dealerships give prospects the opportunity to experience what the new car will be like on a test drive before they buy.

How can you create a more immersive and amazing experience for your prospects *before* they buy?

Sellers who move from transactional to continuity based sales models or who sell on layaway are also selling in an altered way so that products and services can be delivered over time instead of immediately.

When you publish content, you gain leverage. For example, a product created ten years ago can still provide value years later. If you haven't published anything yet, you should start now so that you can be reaping the benefits years and decades from now.

Technology allows you to connect with so many people through social media. You can put up a video on YouTube and create that video one time but can connect with millions of prospects.

Another way that you can create leverage is to repurpose your content. In other words, if you create a video in YouTube, you can also put on Facebook, you can Tweet it, you can put it on Pinterest, etc. The point is that you can get value out of creating an idea one time.

3. Studying and continual commitment to the mastery of the sales process.
How deeply do you study and practice the selling process?

To master something implies that you are working at it all of the time. You aren't content with what you knew before. You keep learning and figuring out what works, and what doesn't.

There are great sales training materials at www.SalesChampion.com that can help you master the sales process. The reality is that there is more resistance in selling today, and if you aren't asking more, you are losing a lot of sales. You are getting the prospect ¾ to almost all of the way sold and then letting her leave so that she is nearly over her resistance to buy. Then, she ends up buying from someone else. Your competitors are thankful because you have worn down a prospect's resistance for them so it is easier for them to make the sale because of your efforts.

Don't make this mistake. Train your sales consultants to ask for the sale at least five times with every sale they make. The sales training available on SalesChampion.com will help you get better and persuading, persisting, and selling more. These tools will help you develop the skills and tenacity to ask for the sale. When you do, you'll see your sales and closing percentages go up and you'll be ecstatic about the result.

A great example of the power of sales mastery can be found in all of the product spokespeople on QVC. Megan McCardle points this out: "The QVC process is so finely calibrated that a producer watches call volume in real time; whenever it spikes, the host hears a voice in his or her ear: "Whatever you just said, say it again. It's working." The lessons are disseminated to other hosts, and to the product spokespeople, who must spend hours training before they may present their products on air.

"QVC has not created any of these techniques; it has only mastered them. Which is why QVC's relationship with its customers tells you a lot about what America has been doing for the past 20 years or so. More and more buying on credit, fewer real-life interactions, a proliferating array of products to tempt us—and of "new media" outlets allowing companies to better target their audiences with parasocial fantasies." –Megan McCardle, The Genius of QVC, http://www.theatlantic.com/magazine/archive/2010/06/the-genius-of-qvc/8091/2/

Another example is that of pitchman Arnold Morris as recounted by Malcolm Gladwell in *The New Yorker*:
"The last of the Morrises to be active in the pitching business is Arnold (the Knife) Morris, so named because of his extraordinary skill with the Sharpcut, the forerunner of the Ginsu. He is in his early seventies, a cheerful, impish man with a round face and a few wisps of white hair, and a trademark move whereby, after cutting a tomato into neat, regular slices, he deftly lines the pieces up in an even row against the flat edge of the blade.... Arnold wasn't merely entertaining; he was selling. "You can take a pitchman and make a great actor out of him, but you cannot take an actor and always make a great pitchman out of him," he says. The pitchman must make you applaud and take out your money. He must be able to execute what in pitchman's

parlance is called "the turn"--the perilous, crucial moment where he goes from entertainer to businessman. If, out of a crowd of fifty, twenty-five people come forward to buy, the true pitchman sells to only twenty of them. To the remaining five, he says, "Wait! There's something else I want to show you!" Then he starts his pitch again, with slight variations, and the remaining four or five become the inner core of the next crowd, hemmed in by the people around them, and so eager to pay their money and be on their way that they start the selling frenzy all over again. The turn requires the management of expectation. That's why Arnold always kept a pineapple tantalizingly perched on his stand. "For forty years, I've been promising to show people how to cut the pineapple, and I've never cut it once," he says. "It got to the point where a pitchman friend of mine went out and bought himself a plastic pineapple. Why would you cut the pineapple? It cost a couple bucks. And if you cut it they'd leave."

"One story that is particularly interesting about the importance of sales mastery:
"Arnold says that he once hired some guys to pitch a vegetable slicer for him at a fair in Danbury, Connecticut, and became so annoyed at their lackadaisical attitude that he took over the demonstration himself. They were, he says, waiting for him to fail: he had never worked that particular slicer before and, sure enough, he was massacring the vegetables. Still, in a single pitch he took in two hundred dollars. "Their eyes popped out of their heads," Arnold recalls. "They said, `We don't understand it. You don't even know how to work the damn machine.' I said, `But I know how to do one thing better than you.' They said, `What's that?' I said, `I know how to ask for the money.' And that's the secret to the whole damn business." -http://gladwell.com/2000/2000_10_30_a_pitchman.htm

What difference in results is there between a staff of trained consultants over those who have little to no training and wing it when they get in front of your prospects? The answer adds up, so be sure that you are continually improving at the process of selling so that you and your team can get the results you want.

4. Game changing elements

Sometimes little things can completely transform the competitive
landscape in a way that shows you how powerful the strategy of
leverage can be. Consider that Disney introduced a single price
admission ticket at a time when many amusement parks were set up in
a way that you entered for free and then paid at each individual ride.
Disney changed all of that by including the purchase of the rides in
the single price admission. Then, they can be sold everything else in
the parks as they pass through a carefully engineered environment
designed to maximize sales. Disney studies the flow of their guests
and how they move within the park. They are constantly monitoring
how many people stop, look in a certain direction, buy, and what they
do in every area of the park. This is all done to maximize the amount
each person spends there. In 2007, Orlando Disney World visitor
surpassed Las Vegas visitor for amount of money spent in 8 hour
period. That is a staggering fact.

Domino's Pizza introduced a game changing strategy that changed the
pizza business with its speed and certainty of delivery guarantee.

A game changing element introduced in many industries is the
concept of fractional ownership. This is a powerful leverage strategy.
This allows multiple people to own a piece of property, a condo, a
private jet, or really expensive jewelry through fractional ownership.

To show the power of leverage, consider this story of how an
expensive piece of jewelry was shared by thirteen women who each
contributed $1200 to buy the necklace. There may be a game-
changing lesson in this story that you could apply in your business.

Here is what author Cheryl Jarvis said in an article she wrote for the
Daily Mail entitled: "The necklace that changed their lives: How 13
women shared a single piece of 15-carat diamond jewelry worth
£26,000

"With 118 diamonds and a £26,000 price tag, it was a necklace
beyond the reach of most ordinary women. But what about sharing it
with friends? Thirteen women did just that - with glorious results

"Jonell McLain was sitting at her desk looking at the piles of paper surrounding her and struggling not to feel overwhelmed. Why were there always 45 things on her to-do list?

"She felt like Sisyphus, the king in the Greek legend who was condemned to push the same rock up a mountain, over and over - some days all she seemed to accomplish was moving mountains of paper.

"Today, however, she was also feeling the high that estate agents get when they complete a deal. This one represented three months of work and emotional exhaustion. People buying homes are always on edge, and because her work was so stressful, Jonell made a point of rewarding herself when each commission check came in.

"She hadn't decided what to buy herself this time, but she headed out anyway. In Ventura, a California beach town 60 miles north of Los Angeles, she walked through the shopping mall. As she passed the window of Van Gundy & Sons - the Tiffany's of Ventura - something stopped her in her tracks.

"In the display case was a necklace glittering against black velvet. The diamonds were strung in a single strand all the way to the clasp; the centre diamond was the largest and the two closest to the clasp the smallest. The gradations were minuscule, the effect breathtaking. Jonell stood and stared.

"She rarely wore good jewelry. She owned diamond wedding rings from two husbands, gold earrings and watches. But luxury jewelry was something else. What would it feel like, she wondered, to wear something so lovely and extravagant?
On a whim she entered the shop. 'Could I see the necklace in the window?' she asked nonchalantly, as if she did this every day.

Tentatively, she tried it on. It was simply exquisite — and exquisitely simple. 118 diamonds, the saleswoman was telling her, Jonell breathed

in, and as she exhaled, she asked the price.
'Thirty-seven thousand dollars.' [£26,000]

"Jonell gasped. All she could think was: 'Who buys a $37,000
necklace?'

"She thought back to the choices she'd made in her life, the ones that
guaranteed she could never afford a necklace like this. How different
things might have been if she'd married a wealthy man or invested
more in a career. Maybe then she could have been able to indulge in
such luxury.
'

But in the end, none of this mattered, not really. In a world
overflowing with need, the idea of owning a $37,000 necklace was, she
told herself, morally indefensible. After admiring it for another
minute, she laid the necklace back on the counter and thanked the
saleswoman for her time.

"It had been a momentary fantasy, but in the weeks that followed,
Jonell couldn't stop thinking about it. Three weeks later, she noticed
the necklace was still in the window, but there was now a sale - the
price had been reduced to $21,000.

"From left-field, an idea took shape in her mind. 'No one woman
needs to have a 15-carat diamond necklace all the time,' she reasoned.
'But wouldn't it be delightful to have one every now and then - a sort
of time-share necklace?'

"Jonell started phoning friends and colleagues. She calculated that she
needed a group of 12 to chip in if the necklace was to be even
remotely affordable. Most, having heard her idea, said no. No money.
No time. No interest in diamonds. Even her mother warned: 'You'll
lose friends over this.'

"But two months later, she had a group of seven. Close enough, she
decided. Van Gundy & Sons were having a one-off auction day,
inviting bids on any item of jewelry on display.

"They could try to get it for $12,000, she told herself, with each woman paying $1,000. She could put the balance on her Visa card and by the time the bill arrived, she'd have found the remaining five women she needed.

"On the Saturday of the auction, Jonell and her friends arrived early at Van Gundy's to beat any competing bidders.

"They preened and giggled and it was obvious to shop owner Tom Van Gundy that these giddy women didn't buy diamonds every day.

"Each of them posed for a photo with the necklace and when they finished, Jonell handed Tom an envelope with their bid. Her posture was confident and her smile playful, but she was nervous. In offering $12,000, she was asking him to cut his price in half.

"Tom, meanwhile, was mesmerized by Jonell and her friends. In a quarter of a century of working in the business, he couldn't recall a single woman ever buying luxury jewelry for herself.

"Women fuelled the desire, but they waited for men to make the purchase. When he saw their bid, he winced inwardly. 'I need to look at the figures,' he told them.

"In the back room, Priscilla, his wife and chief financial officer, was hunched over the books. She had heard the commotion but hadn't left her desk to look. Priscilla avoided looking at customers' faces. She didn't want negotiations to get personal.

"'There's a group of women who want a special price on the diamond necklace,' said Tom. 'What can we sell it for?'

"Priscilla tapped figures on the adding machine.

"'Eighteen thousand,' she said.

"Tom knew the number wasn't going to be acceptable, but went back to tell Jonell.

"'Not low enough,' Jonell said. He nodded his head and returned to the back room.

"'Can we go lower?' he asked Priscilla. She felt his apprehension.

""Thirty-three years of marriage and she could read his emotions like a spreadsheet.

"'Seventeen thousand,' she answered. Tom scribbled '$15,000,' and showed it to Priscilla.

"'Can we do this?' he asked.

"'That's ridiculous,' answered Priscilla.

"'It could be good for business,' said Tom.

"'We sell it for that and we won't have a business,' replied Priscilla.

"Tom looked at his wife. She had her finger on every dollar, and he trusted her more than anyone. But today he wanted her to be flexible. 'I have a feeling about this,' he said. At that moment, Tom Van Gundy realized he was willing to let go of any profit. Deep down, he wanted to see his wife smile the way these women were smiling.

"'I'll give it to you for $15,000,' he told Jonell, 'on one condition. I want you to let my wife be in your group.'

"He had no idea how Priscilla would feel about it. He just knew he wanted these women in her life.

"'It's a deal,' said Jonell.

"Jonell and her friends sailed out of Van Gundy's each having agreed to pay $1,200 and with Jonell saying a quick prayer and doing some fast mental arithmetic: with Priscilla, they were now a group of eight, but she would still need to find another five women to invest.

"Later, at home, Jonell put the diamonds on and realized, that the necklace was perfect for her. Her blonde hair, her frameless glasses, her minimalist make-up - the necklace looked good with all of it. No question, she thought, this is amazing.

"Meanwhile, back at Van Gundy's, Tom confessed the terms of his deal to his wife.

"Priscilla knew that he felt bad about dropping the price, so held back the tetchy retorts that filled her head. Had he lost his mind? They wouldn't even cover their costs.

"She had no curiosity about the women and no interest in owning a necklace she could have borrowed any time she wanted.

"But Tom Van Gundy had seen something his wife hadn't. He'd seen a group of women unlike any others he'd ever come across - and he'd seen possibility.

"Jonell's vision wasn't about diamonds as a status or investment. It was about a necklace as a cultural experiment. A way to bring 13 adventurous women together to see what would happen.

"And her confidence wasn't misplaced. By the time her Visa bill arrived three weeks later, she'd found the final five investors she needed.

"Apart from the jeweler's disgruntled wife, there were old friends, new friends and friends of friends. Now they were 13 - a diverse group whose ages ranged from 50 to 62. Some had long-standing marriages, others had had two or three husbands and dozens of lovers. Some were childless while the rest had up to four children.

"Between them, they worked in finance and farming, medicine and teaching, business and property, media and law. Some came from wealthy families and others were completely self-made.

"None of the women had said 'yes' to Jonell's proposition because they were interested in diamonds. Each bought a share because it represented an unexpected opportunity.

"What the women didn't know was that over the next three years the necklace would animate their lives in ways they could never have imagined.

"This is the story of a necklace, but it isn't the story of a string of stones. It's the story of 13 women who transformed a symbol of exclusivity into a symbol of inclusivity and, in the process, remapped the journey of their lives.

"Jonell's first email to her fellow investors read as follows: 'It's about time we got this fabulous group together. Let's meet on Thursday at 4pm. Please come prepared to talk about the necklace's name, how to divide up the time, insurance, and anything else that seems fun, relevant or not - I can't wait to see what happens next.'

"Priscilla Van Gundy read the email. She was busy as usual. 'Who's got time for a meeting with a bunch of women?' she thought. Her reply was terse: 'I won't be able to make it. I have to work.' She and Tom were overhauling the shop and Priscilla was working 60 hours a week. She was beginning to feel like the Bill Murray character in the film Groundhog Day: every morning, even on Sunday, she woke up to the same life, the same grind. Last year she'd taken just 12 days off. The pace had been gruelling. Now, one of the store managers had handed in his notice, which meant she would have to deal with customers. She found selling exhausting - so many women wanting to talk. The same two or three trudged in every week with their slumped shoulders, their sad eyes. Their husbands had died or left them. Their children were out of town or out of touch.

"Priscilla knew they were shopping just to fill their days. They didn't

want a watch or a ring. They wanted a friend and their loneline
palpable.

"Priscilla knew something of how lost they felt. She had a job, a
husband and three grown-up children who lived nearby, but just a few
months earlier, her sister, Doreen, had died from a rare form of cancer.
'Doreen was the life of our family,' says Priscilla, 57. 'With her death I
shut down completely. I got up and did what I had to do, but I was
just going through the motions.

"'After work each night I'd go straight to the bedroom, put on my
pajamas, and climb into bed to watch American Idol or Seinfeld. I
shut off from everyone, even my husband.

"'I'm good at isolating myself. I've done it my whole life. But there
comes a time when you realize you've spent too much time alone.'

"The eldest of six children, Priscilla grew up in a tough Hispanic
community surrounded by gang culture. Her parents - her father was
a builder, her mother a cleaner - strived to send her to a good school,
where she often felt a gulf between herself and her classmates.

"'I remember a conversation where we were talking about what we
wanted for Christmas. I said I needed a coat. One of the girls said
scornfully: "Why don't you ask for something you want?" But I was
lucky to get what I needed. They couldn't understand my world, and I
couldn't understand theirs.

"'I thought it'd be the same thing with the necklace women. I didn't
think I was in their league.'

"When Jonell's second email dropped a couple of weeks later, Priscilla
learnt that the women had named the necklace Jewelia (pronounced
Julia). They had also established a time-share arrangement in which
each woman would have the necklace for 28 days. 'Mary and Priscilla,
we missed you,' Jonell wrote. Priscilla stared at her computer. Could

she be missing something?

"When the date of the next meeting was set, Priscilla decided that if she was going to attend, she should try to make a good impression. She put on her best suit and designer high heels.

"Her jewelry she didn't worry about: one of the perks of owning a jewelry shop was that she could borrow whatever she wanted. (The downside was that nothing was really hers. If a customer admired her jewelry and wanted to buy it, she took it off that day and never wore it again.)

"She found a place to park outside the restaurant where the meeting was being held and braced herself. Inside, the single chair at the long, rectangular table loudly indicated she was the last to arrive. 'I'm sorry I'm late,' she said, rushing the words. 'I had work to take care of.'

"Jonell jumped out of her seat, wrapped an arm around her and introduced her to the others. Everyone broke into huge smiles. Priscilla sat down. She knew it wasn't polite, but she couldn't help staring at the blonde woman across from her who was wearing a leopard print jersey wrapped snugly and suggestively around her body.

"Priscilla didn't know that women in their 50s could look that good. Had they had an indepth conversation, Priscilla would have discovered that, unlike her, Maggie Hood had had three husbands and many friends over the years. But they also had lots in common. Two thousand miles from Ventura, in the inner city of Chicago, Maggie had also had a tough start in life.

"Maggie smiled warmly at Priscilla and Priscilla smiled back. Then she found her eyes drawn to another woman with cascading blonde hair who was wearing the diamond necklace.

"For more than a year, Priscilla had seen the necklace in the shop every day, but she'd never seen it look the way it looked today. The brilliance of the diamonds cast an aura around not just the woman's face but her whole being.

"Priscilla believed in signs. The first time she'd laid eyes on Tom Van Gundy she knew in that moment he was the man she was going to marry. She felt something powerful happening here, too. She wanted to belong.

"That night, Tom saw Priscilla smile for the first time in a long time. 'It's a great group of women,' Priscilla said. 'Thank you for making me part of it.'

"'I didn't do anything,' said Tom.
"'Of course you did,' said Priscilla.
'I just saw those women having so much fun together and I wanted that for you,' said Tom.
"'I didn't realize how much I wasn't like that,' said Priscilla.
'You used to be,' said Tom.

"'Before meeting these women,' recalls Priscilla, 'I was always saying "no". Tom would ask me for a lower price, like he did with the diamond necklace, and I'd say "no". He'd ask me if I wanted to go to Hawaii and I'd say "we can't afford it".

"'When my daughter went on trips with her girlfriends, I'd give her a hard time. I sucked the life out of everyone around me.

"'Going to the meetings was the beginning of my saying "yes". The group was the greatest gift my husband ever gave me. He gave me my life back.'" --http://www.dailymail.co.uk/femail/article-1138353/The-necklace-changed-lives-How-13-women-shared-single-piece-15-carat-diamond-jewellery-worth-26-000.html#ixzz13eQtO5WI

What did you learn from this story about the power of leverage?

How could you incorporate that idea into your life?

In what ways would that transform what you do?

In his book *The Millionaire Mind*, Thomas J. Stanley points out: "It's rare that anyone becomes successful without the assistance of others. A group of individuals, no matter how gifted, is not a team at all. How many running backs became All-Americans without their linemen opening up opportunities? Zero. Becoming wealthy in America is very similar. I have never met one affluent person who takes complete credit for his economic successes. Most will give credit to their spouse, key employees, mentors, and others. No man or woman is an island, whether the context is sports, business, or building wealth—nobody gets to the highest peaks without the help of others."—*The Millionaire Mind*, p. 37.

Those who reach the highest realms of success employ the leverage of others to help them get there faster.

Jay Abraham shares this story in his book *Getting Everything You Can Out of All You've Got* about the importance of having the right multiplier to fuel growth. He said: "At one of my training programs a few years back I had speaking for me a prominent and respected expert in advertising. He was trying to make a very powerful point...He asked the audience a really interesting question. He said, 'Let's presume we're going to go into the restaurant business and each one of us can choose the one advantage we could have over everyone else. We're going to go into Los Angeles and you get to pick the first advantage before I do. What are you going to pick?'

"And he went around and let every participant choose the one factor they thought would give them the greatest success. When he was done he said, 'Fine. Now let me tell you the one factor I want. I want a starving crowd.' The lesson: The right list will connect you with your starving crowd." –pp. 269-270.

If you could have one advantage over anyone else in your business, what would it be? What would be the single multiplier you would like to have if you could have just one?

What would be the single leverage point that would give you the most power to propel your growth ahead of any and all of your competitors?

This is a valuable exercise to contemplate. Once you've identified your differentiating point, you can utilize it to dominate your market.

5. Sell to more affluent markets.

In today's economy, it is critically important that you learn to better market to affluent prospects and clients. Why? The reason is that there is much more resilience in spending now with the affluent, that you won't find with many prospects today who have tighter and more constrained budgets.

In the height of the Great Recession according to Bain Capital's Milan-based fashion luxury investment team, 2010 global sales of luxury goods...exceed[ed] $237 billion (which is up over the $214 billion sold in 2009). Burberry and Louis Vuitton reported double digit sales increases in the 3rd quarter of [2010]. Similar occurrences in markets and niches across the world have found the same trend in the past several years.

What this means is that you should be focusing in on and targeting the affluent population in order to sell more of what you sell in the year to come. It is important to market where the money is.

Recent statistics revealed that 22% of the U.S. households have over 55% of all earned income. This means that more than half of income is concentrated in 1 of 5 households. If you study what great companies are doing, they are focusing in on creating unique experiences for the affluent so that they can draw them into their businesses and be more successful as a result.

Here are five benefits to selling to more prospects and clients:

1) *You can grow quickly with faster speed (fewer transactions, higher transaction size)*

2) You will be more profitable which will give you a powerful sustainable advantage because you can now spend more to acquire additional prospects and customers.

3) You can reach your personal goals faster because you can take profits out of your business to create your own personal financial independence.

4) There are fewer competitors in this space because most entrepreneurs don't gravitate to higher prices, they usually gravitate to the lowest resistance and seek to sell for lower prices. That means there is opportunity if you focus on this for you.

5) You can provide a more superior experience for your customers so that your experience is more amazing. As a result, you will become the dominant, preferred, celebrated business in your market niche and other prospects will seek you out because you can provide the best possible experience.

So, how can you better market to affluent individuals? Here are some things for you to consider:

Do you segment your list so that you send out your marketing collateral to areas where the most affluent in your community live (and those who are most likely to buy higher priced products and services that you offer)? If not, you are making a big mistake. It is so important to target your message of buying a premium experience to the market who can best afford and utilize what it is that you are selling.

A good question to ask yourself is this: Which kinds of customers do you want? Those who can easily afford and pay up front for what you sell? Or those who have can barely make their payments each and every month? The answer of course is that you would love to be able to serve both markets, but it makes much more sense to sell to the segment of the market who can best afford the experiences **and** the products you sell.

The other big lesson from the statistics I shared earlier about how spending has surged in the luxury categories in the past year is that the number of consumers who purchased these items actually decreased.

That means that the way you select your customers (or in other words who and how you market your business) is absolutely critical to your survival. Your business can't succeed if you just throw marketing dollars at the wall and hope something sticks long enough to bring prospects into your marketing funnel. Instead, you must be much more sophisticated about how you spend your marketing money and much more targeted in your approach so you attract prospects who not only *can* spend money with you, but are *willing to spend more with you* to get the very best experience and product possible.

Another interested statistic by Luxury Institute indicates that 36% of luxury buyers are less willing to pay premium prices for luxury products today because of the perceived loss of quality or service differential. In other words, to woo affluent buyers today, you had better deliver what you say you will. There is less tolerance today for anything less than extraordinary.

Remember, the competition is anyone the customer compares you with. In other words, any business that prospects compare you with is your competition. This expanded view of who your competition should shift how you look at your business. The experience they have there likely is reflected on how they view you. Here are three questions for you to think about regarding this principle and to think about how you are marketing to and perceived by the affluent prospects in your market niche.

- Think about a recent experience you had with exceptional customer service at another business. How did that experience raise your expectations of what other companies do and what you should be doing better in your business?
- How does your service compare to other businesses affluent clients are familiar with?

- What does that suggest about how you might change the way you do business?

Grant Miller, owns a chain of five upscale tanning salons called Sun Your Buns in Erie, Pennsylvania. We recently talked about our businesses and he shared the benefits he has found by marketing better to the affluent. Grant's average prices are much higher than his local competitors and even national averages of other tanning salons. He focuses on the experience his customers have at his salons and shares the benefits members of his V.I.P. Sun Club have (and offers them multiple levels of experiences, themes, and stratification within his business so his customers have a sense of control of what they are buying from him).

Grant's tiered pricing allows him to offer tanning services at his salon from low pricing ($18.88 per month) to very high pricing ($98.88 per month) based on the type of tanning bed they get and the type of overall experience they'll have. Grant has many segments that he markets to and brings into his salons. He markets to teens, young women, professional career women, and affluent women. For each segment he brings into his salon, he has a different type of marketing to best match what he sells with what his customer base is looking for.

This is an important lesson. Very few marketers segment their list this way. They just try to market what they sell to everybody. The reality is that each prospect can be marketed to and sold in a different way if you know where they are coming from and why type of product, service, or solution that they are looking for. It takes much more work to market this way, but the results are nothing short of astonishing.

There are tremendous lessons to learn from better segmenting your marketing to attract more affluent prospects to buy from you. Be sure you are offering experiences to different segments of the market that speak to what is most important to them and give them a sense of control so they can choose what they want without having to feel excluded in any way. No matter how long this trend lasts in your market, those who work harder to market to the affluent clientele who have more resilience to changes in the market will be the ones who rise to the top in their individual market niches.

6. Use the power of celebrity.

Celebrity is a powerful leverage point and multiplier. More than one successful individual that if they were to start their businesses all over again and they could only use one marketing multiplier that it would be to use the power of celebrity because they could leverage the contacts and the influence that these individuals have to grow their social proof and business.

To illustrate the power of celebrity, I'd like to share the successes of Juicy Couture, the power of celebrity endorsements by Oprah Winfrey and how Walt Disney successfully uses celebrities in their business.

"Juicy Couture did not advertise until 2004. Instead, the [founders Gela Nash-Taylor and Pam Skaist-Levy]...brilliantly used the culture of celebrity to sell their brand, sending out free customized Juicy Couture to people they knew could further their cause, particularly targeting movie stars and fashion editors. This approach, known as swag marketing, is not a new approach by any means, but the Juicys took this to another level. Rose Apodaca, West Coash Bureau Chief of WWD, says, "They really know how to work it in terms of getting free product into the hands of people." The Juicy approach was more than sending out a parcel of goodies; they would take a suite at a five-star Los Angeles hotel and have people come through all day—celebrities, editors, assistants, and other key clients, handing out freebies that they would go away and wear, inadvertently promoting Juicy to a wide audience. The exclusivity of the events also added to the buzz about the brand. These events typically cost $20,000 - $100,000 to stage but the return on investment was considerable with reams and reams of editorial coverage. Nash-Taylor says that while their address books are rather impressive, with the likes of Valentino and Oprah Winfrey—both Juicy wearers—she says that they like the Juicy product for the same reason that their non-famous clients do. Nash-Taylor points out: 'No amount of Madonnas can sell a product that isn't good.'

"In fact in 2001, they launched their range of velour, low-cut, comfy tracksuits. "They were a fashion phenomenon with Madonna, Oprah, and many other celebrities wearing custom Juicy Couture tracksuits. Paparazzi shots of Juicy clad off-duty celebrities appeared in glossy magazines around the world, and a new, velour star was born." --*100 Great Businesses and the Minds Behind Them*, pp. 336-337.

Now, you may say, that you don't know any celebrities. You can get to know some in your local area if you work at it, and more importantly you can create celebrities out of your own customer base by profiling them in a monthly newsletter or by conducting contests where the winners become celebrities because of how you promote them.

Resources are available for you to find out and align your business with celebrities today. A great resource that you can get is Jordan McAuley's book: *The Celebrity Black Book: Over 60,000+ Accurate Celebrity Addresses for Autographs, Charity Donations, Signed Memorabilia, Celebrity Endorsements, Media Interviews and More!*

Many entrepreneurs have successfully utilized the power of celebrity to leverage huge crowds of people during product launches. You can do the same.

There is no question that celebrities permeate our culture and have a tremendous power if they are utilized correctly. You may want to consider aligning yourself with a celebrity to help you promote your business in your own local area. You also definitely want to promote yourself as a big part of your brand so that you are building your own celebrity.

Walt Disney understood the power of celebrities. He chose his friend Art Linkletter to host the television show where he launched Disneyland. Linkletter recommended to Disney that he also use two co-hosts since they would be broadcasting from around the park. These two individuals were popular actor Robert Cummings and future president Ronald Reagan. He also had Disney stars Fess Parker and Buddy Ebsen perform songs from the 'Davy Crockett' television episodes. Frank Sinatra was there, as were numerous other well-known celebrities of the day. Disney also used the event to create future celebrities out of the Mousketeers who he had at his side of the opening of the theme park (whose show would premiere on October 3rd of that year).

7. Be more profitable. Profit is the biggest multiplier and leverage point of all in business.
So, how do you increase your profitability? Here are eight ways:

1. Raise prices.
If you haven't raised your prices in a while, it is time to do so. But, don't just raise your prices. Raise your value of what it is that you offer in the marketplace.

2. Change who you are selling to.
The key is to sell to more affluent markets, to those accustomed or even eager to pay premium prices. The reality is that to the affluent, price doesn't affect how they buy. In fact, the more expensive, the better it is since it validates their status.

What happens when you sell at low prices and low profit margins? Here are four results:
- You have less power and are weaker. Why? The answer is that you can only spend the bare minimum (or very little) to get prospects into your business
  - You have to settle for slow growth since you have no money to reinvest in products that could maximize your profitability and you can't spend more to get more customers in the door.
  - The experience you provide in your business is ordinary and average. You can't afford to provide fun surprises for prospects and so your biggest problem becomes that your product, service, or experience can be easily duplicated by your competitors so that in the end, what you all offer becomes the same in the eyes of your prospects.

- You are limited in building your long-term wealth because with fewer profits, it is much more challenging to build long-term equity in your business and build your financial independence and wealth over a sustained period of time.

3. Charge for what you now provide for free & others in the industry (including your competitors) still do
I have discussed this before, but the key lesson here is this: What others choose to give away for free at their businesses is irrelevant to what you do in your business. Increase your profit by charging for things (or raising the price to include things that you used to provide for free).

4. Force a higher transaction size by bundling accessories into the sale – we include our princess package with the purchase price of the dress (if they buy on the first visit)

5. Look for opportunities to sell things after the first sale.
For examples, hair dressers offer hair and beauty products after their first sale (the haircut). Carpet cleaners offer repeat visits or the opportunity to clean more rooms in your home or business. When you buy a car, you are sold options after you purchase the car (alarm, treatment under your car and on your seats, etc.)

How can you upsell after your first sale?

The key to successfully answering and acting on that question lies in how you look to continue to provide value to your clients after you have already gained their trust. Look for ways you can get paid in repeatable ways for what you do and how you do it. This is a powerful idea of how to utilize leverage in your business.

6. Change the way you sell. Your goal should be to get better at selling on the first visit because it decreases your cost of customer acquisition and allows you to be more profitable.

7. Change what you sell. Choose to sell what allows you to make money. Remember, you are in control of what you offer to others.

How can you stretch the price pyramid in your business and offer more high value products to your clients?

8. Build more value into what you sell.
A great example of a business who is doing this well is Nationwide. They have created a phone app which allows their customers to document an accident with an interactive walk through and step-by-step guide so that any customer can complete the process. If you are in an accident, you can take pictures then and there of your car, the crash scene, the other car, and each of your license plates. Then, customers can hit a button and submit the claim then and there. This is a great way they've added more value to their customers and a way they are standing out from their competitors.

8. Be unique. What kind of leverage does being the same offer vs. being unique?
One of the reasons why Trader Joe's has been so successful is because they understand this principle and strive to dominate their market niche. A great book by Len Lewis entitled *The Trader Joe's Adventure: Turning a Unique Approach to Business into a Retail and Cultural Phenomenon* would be great for you to study if you want more information on what they are doing in their business to stand out and be unique. In the book, Lewis lists the following six ways (and there are many more ways in the book) that Trader Joe's is able to leverage their assets to accomplish more than their competitors. These include:

o *Having proprietary brands that no one else does.*

o *They work hard to satisfy their suppliers* – "If you ask suppliers, many will tell you that Trader Joe's is their most efficient and profitable customers. Moreover, once you hit the company's specs and meet its price expectations, executives...trust suppliers to do what they were contracted to do, enabling the chain to run a lean and more profitable organization. In some ways, Trader Joe's operates on the same principles as Wal-Mart but without the hard-line buying strategy that squeezes every last penny out of vendors. They want what they want and pay fairly and regularly. 'They don't cause vendors anywhere near the headache of a regular supermarket,' says Alex Lintner of The Boston Consulting Group in San Francisco. 'They don't want slotting or promotional allowances, just the best price. And if you deliver it, they'll make sure they sell it.'—*The Trader Joe's Adventure*, p. 43.

o *The seek high profit margins and "concentrate on the fastest-*selling items from one or two suppliers that can be handled efficiently." –p. 44.

o *They constantly seek out unique items they can sell.* "[Trader Joe's] is out there scouring the market for unique items. If they can get popcorn from some obscure place or licorice from Australia and get exclusive rights to it, that's what they are going to do.'—p. 46.

o *They leverage their buying power.*

o *Speed to market.* "At present Trader Joe's is constantly replacing existing items on variations—tweaking the mix. The company introduces 20 to 25 products a week, and 'sometimes we're right, and sometimes we're not. If we're not, we don't order it again and we let it run out...Sometimes, that makes customers unhappy.'—p. 47

Are you constantly looking at what is selling and replacing it with more of the same and eliminating what isn't selling for you?

The most important area to be unique in is what you offer to your prospects, or in other words the products you sell. You can't have what everyone else has. You have to be unique and be different. I really like what the late Steve Jobs said about this. He said: "In the market place, Apple is trying to focus the spotlight on products, because products really make a difference...Ad campaigns are necessary for competition; IBM's ads are everywhere. But good PR educates people; that's all it is. You can't con people in this business. The products speak for themselves."

If you can't have exclusivity with a product, you are giving up a significant leverage point and multiplier. When you have a product, your prospects can fall in love with and can't get anywhere else, you have a tremendous amount of leverage and power.
What market gaps do you see in your market niche?

What unmet needs or desires do prospects and clients have?

How could you meet those?

How could this set you apart from your competitors?

9. **Look closely at the processes in your business and how you can improve them. Improved processes can be little hinges that swing big doors and offer great leverage.**
There are several ways you can change the processes in your business to have more leverage. You can bundle accessories, you can move from a single sale to a continuity model. You can raise your prices by adding more value. Here is an example of the power of raising your prices by $100 based on how many products you sell:
- $100 increase x 1000 products = $100,000 more gross profit
- $100 increase x 500 products = $50,000 more gross profit
- $100 increase x 200 products = $20,000 more gross profit

What processes can you improve in your business to better leverage what you sell?

Here are some questions you could ask:

- How is the phone answered? Could you change the way you invite prospects to do business with you on the phone?
- What do prospects experience during the first 30 seconds after they walk through your doors or enter your marketing funnel?
- What do prospects experience on their first visit?
- How can you better target prospects who don't buy from you in the first visit?
  i. Know your marketing sequence in advance
  ii. What bait will entice prospects to return back to your marketing funnel?
  iii. How can you invite prospects to return? Do you have a good follow-up system?
  iv. Could you offer a weekly, monthly, or quarterly newsletter to remind your prospects about you and have them return to do business with you? Here is a minimum of six things your newsletter could include:
     1. Featured client of the month
     2. Featured product of the month
     3. Details about what you've been up to and how you're serving clients now
     4. Featured event of the month and turn this into a reason why your prospect should return and buy now
     5. What the trends are...what types of products are popular and what they may not have considered as they have been searching for what you sell
     6. Answers to questions from prospects and clients

Our hope is that you'll use the ideas we've shared with you here to leverage your time and your business to even greater success as you consider new opportunities or better capitalize on existing opportunities you may have forgotten about or aren't implementing as well as you could.

ABOUT THE AUTHORS:

Eric Lofholm is a master sales trainer who has helped over 10,000 students make more sales. Trained by best-selling sales expert Dr. Donald Moine, Eric has helped generate nearly $500 million in revenue in the last two decades. Eric honed his skills as a sales trainer for Tony Robbins from 1997 to 1999 before founding his own company, Eric Lofholm International. He offers expert training for both corporate sales departments and for individuals who want to improve their sales skills.

He is the author of the #1 best-selling book *The System*. You can get your copy at: http://www.amazon.com/System-Proven-3-Step-Formula-Appointments/dp/0989894207/ref=sr_1_1?ie=UTF8&qid=1421081452&sr=8-1&keywords=Eric+Lofholm+The+System
Eric is also the publisher of the I Love Selling Magazine and the I Love Selling Podcast. He is the father of two children.

Visit Eric's web site at www.SalesChampion.com

James Karl Butler is a serial entrepreneur who has built four companies from the start-up phase to over a million dollars in revenue. He is the author of eight books and numerous E-books. He grew his first retail bridal store from $0 to over $1,000,000 in sales in three years and grew another retail business from $0 to over $1,000,000 in just over 18 months. James has helped some of the most respected and largest retailers and businesses across the country to grow their sales and shatter their previous sales records. He is a celebrated systems and marketing authority who speaks and trains business owners how to create rapid and sustained growth in their business.

He is the author of the best-selling book *The System is the Secret*. You can get your copy here: http://www.amazon.com/System-Secret-Implement-Transform-Business/dp/0578125358/ref=sr_1_1?ie=UTF8&qid=1421081775&sr=8-1&keywords=James+Karl+Butler+The+System+is+the+Secret
He is the host of the Sound Laws of Success Podcast and inspires entrepreneurs to take action in their businesses through applying these laws. He and his wife Heather are the parents of five children.

Visit his web site at: www.SoundLawsofSuccess.com

77266264R00028

Made in the USA
Columbia, SC
18 September 2017